D1597812

ENJOY WITHOUT SOY

Easy and Delicious Soya-free Recipes
for Kids With Allergies

by **KATRINA JORGENSEN**

CONSULTANT
Amy Durkan MS, RDN, CDN
Nutrition Research Manager
Mount Sinai Medical Center
New York, NY, USA

raintree
a Capstone company — publishers for children

Raintree is an imprint of Capstone Global Library Limited, a company incorporated in England and Wales having its registered office at 264 Banbury Road, Oxford, OX2 7DY – Registered company number: 6695582

www.raintree.co.uk
myorders@raintree.co.uk

Edited by Anna Butzer
Designed by Heidi Thompson
Picture research by Morgan Walters
Production by Kathy McColley

ISBN 978 1 4747 1070 1
20 19 18 17 16
10 9 8 7 6 5 4 3 2 1

British Library Cataloguing in Publication Data
A full catalogue record for this book is available from the British Library.

Design Elements
Shutterstock: avian, design element, Katerina Kirilova, design element, Lena Pan, design element, Marco Govel, design element, mexrix, design element, Sabina Pittak, design element, STILLFX, design element, swatchandsoda, design element

Photography by Capstone Studio: Karon Dubke

Editor's note:
Capstone cannot ensure that any food is allergen-free. The only way to be sure a food is safe is to read all labels carefully, every time. Cross-contamination is also a risk for those with food allergies. Please phone food companies to make sure their manufacturing processes avoid cross-contamination. Also, always make sure you clean hands, surfaces and tools before cooking.

Printed in China.

CONTENTS

WHAT IS A FOOD ALLERGY?

Our bodies are armed with immune systems. It's the immune system's job to fight infections, viruses and invaders. Sometimes the immune system identifies a particular food as one of these invaders and attacks it. While our immune system fights, a chemical response is triggered and causes an allergic reaction. Reactions vary greatly from a mild skin irritation to having trouble breathing. Whenever you feel you are having a reaction, tell an adult immediately.

The best way to avoid having an allergic reaction is to be aware of what you are eating. Be careful not to consume that allergen. If you are not sure if that allergen is in a food, ask an adult or read the ingredients label of the food container before eating. Unfortunately, allergens can sometimes be hard to identify in an ingredient list. Have a look at www.allergyuk.org/soya-and-soy-allergy/soya-soy-allergy for a full list of hidden soya terms.

Avoiding food allergens can be hard to do, especially when they are found in so many of our favourite foods. This cookbook will take you on a culinary journey to explore many of the dishes you've had to avoid because of a soya allergy.

Kitchen safety

A safe kitchen is a fun kitchen! Always start your recipes with clean hands, surfaces and tools. Wash your hands and any tools you may use in future steps of a recipe, especially when handling raw meat. Make sure you have an adult nearby to help you with any task you don't feel comfortable doing, such as cutting vegetables or carrying hot pans.

ALLERGY ALERTS AND TIPS

Have other food allergies? No problem.
Have a look at the list at the end of each recipe
for substitutions for other common allergens.
Look out for other cool tips and ideas too!

CONVERSIONS

1/4 teaspoon	1.25 grams or millilitres
1/2 teaspoon	2.5 g or mL
1 teaspoon	5 g or mL
1 tablespoon	15 g or mL
10 grams	1/3 ounce
50 grams	1 3/4 oz
100 grams	3 1/2 oz
455 grams	16 oz (1 pound)
10 mL	1/3 fluid oz
50 mL	1 3/4 fl oz
100 mL	3 1/2 fl oz

Fahrenheit (°F)	Celsius (°C)
325°	160°
350°	180°
375°	190°
400°	200°
425°	220°
450°	230°

CHERRY PIE BREAKFAST
BARS

Pie for breakfast? It may sound like an early morning dessert, but these bars can give you a nutritious start to your day. The dates and cherries provide a sweet flavour without adding sugar.

Preparation time: 2 hours 15 minutes (2 hours inactive)

Makes 8 bars

Ingredients

90 grams pitted dates

2 tablespoons water

100 grams rolled oats

90 grams dried cherries

Tools

food processor

measuring spoons/scales

medium baking tray

baking parchment

chef's knife

Allergen alert!

Make sure you check the label of your rolled oats if you're allergic to wheat.

Many dried fruits and dates are manufactured with nuts. Make sure you check with the manufacturer to ensure they are safe for you.

1. Combine the dates and water in a food processor. Pulse until the mixture is mostly smooth.

2. Add the rolled oats. Then turn food processor on high for about 30 seconds.

3. Put the cherries in the food processor bowl and pulse about 10 times. The cherries should be chunky.

4. Line the baking tray with baking parchment. Press the dough mixture into the pan with your hands, making sure it is spread out evenly.

5. Place in freezer for two hours to set.

6. Remove from freezer and allow to thaw slightly, about 15 minutes. Slice into eight bars.

7. Store leftovers in refrigerator in an airtight container for up to two weeks.

CHEF'S TIP

Does cherry pie make you squirm?
Any dried fruits can be used.
Try apples, apricots, pineapple
or even mango instead!

HOMEMADE TOASTER
PASTRIES

You can have a fruit-filled blast by making toaster pastries from scratch, and you don't even need a toaster! Packaged breakfast foods at the supermarket might include soya, but these tasty pastries are soya free.

Preparation time: 30 minutes

Cooking time: 30 minutes

Makes 8 pastries

Ingredients

250 grams plain flour, plus a bit more for rolling out the dough

1 tablespoon caster sugar

½ teaspoon salt

225 grams shortening

60 millilitres cold water

80 grams your favourite jam

Icing

140 grams icing sugar

2 tablespoons rice milk

1 teaspoon vanilla extract

Tools

large baking tray

baking parchment

large mixing bowl

measuring spoons/scales/jug

fork

rolling pin

pizza cutter

spatula

small mixing bowl

Allergen alert!

If you need to avoid wheat, use wheat-free flour mix instead.

1. Preheat oven to 180°C. Line a baking tray with baking parchment and set aside.

2. In a mixing bowl, combine the flour, sugar and salt. Using a fork, mix in the shortening until it becomes crumbly, like wet sand.

3. Add water and mix gently with fingers until a dough ball forms. Add water if it's too dry.

4. Sprinkle a couple of tablespoons of flour on a clean surface and place the dough ball on it. Use the rolling pin to flatten the ball into a rectangle about 0.3 centimetre (⅛ inch) thick.

5. Cut 16, 8 x 13-centimetre (3 x 5-inch) rectangles using the pizza cutter. Space evenly on the baking tray about 2.5 centimetres (1 inch) apart.

6. Spread 1 tablespoon of jam on eight of the dough rectangles, leaving about 0.6 centimetre (¼ inch) of space from the edges.

7. Place the plain dough rectangles over the jam-filled rectangles. Press the tines of the fork around the edges to seal.

8. Using the fork, poke a few holes in the top of each pastry. Then place the baking tray in the oven for about 20 minutes, or until the pastries are golden brown. Allow to cool for 10 minutes before icing.

9. Combine all icing ingredients in a mixing bowl. Stir well with a fork until smooth.

10. Ice the pastries by dipping a fork into the icing bowl and drizzling it over the pastries.

11. Store leftovers in the freezer for up to one month. To reheat, place in oven at 180°C for about five minutes.

APPLE PUFF
CEREAL

Start off your day with a bowl of apple cinnamon delight! These sweet puffs have a crunchy outside and a light, airy inside. Unlike many cereals from the supermarket, this recipe will keep soya away from the breakfast table.

Preparation time: 15 minutes

Cooking time: 15 minutes

Makes about 1 bowl of cereal

Ingredients

125 grams plain flour

¼ teaspoon salt

1 teaspoon vanilla extract

½ teaspoon honey

½ teaspoon ground cinnamon

2 tablespoons apple sauce

½ tablespoon olive oil

Tools

large baking tray

baking parchment

food processor

measuring spoons/scales

spatula

1. Preheat oven to 180°C. Line a baking tray with baking parchment and set aside.

2. In a food processor set on high, combine all ingredients until a dough forms.

3. Remove the dough from the food processor with a spatula. Using clean hands, roll the dough into small balls, about the size of a grape.

4. Place the puffs about 2.5 centimetres (1 inch) apart on the baking tray.

5. Put the baking tray in the oven and bake for about seven minutes. Take out the baking tray and swirl it around to roll the puffs over. Return tray to oven to finish baking for an additional eight minutes.

6. Remove from the oven and allow to cool completely before placing in an airtight container.

7. Serve with your favourite milk for breakfast or a snack!

CHEF'S TIP

Don't just eat this with milk for breakfast!
Make a parfait with layers of creamy yogurt,
fresh fruit and crunchy apple puffs!

CHICKEN STEW

Juicy chicken and tender vegetables combine to tantalize your taste buds in this creamy recipe. Heat up the hob for a hearty stew that will fill you up!

Preparation time: 15 minutes

Cooking time: 30 minutes

Serves 4

Ingredients

2 chicken breasts

1 tablespoon oil, such as olive oil

1 small onion

1 stalk celery

1 tablespoon butter

2 tablespoons plain flour

960 millilitres chicken broth

240 millilitres milk

455 grams frozen vegetable mix

1 teaspoon salt

½ teaspoon ground black pepper

Tools

chopping board

chef's knife

measuring spoons/scales/jug

frying pan

tongs

large stockpot

spoon

Allergen alert!

Milk and butter are a no-go if you're avoiding dairy, but no worries! Just use coconut or rice milk instead of ordinary milk. Soya-free, non-dairy butter will work instead of butter.

If you cannot eat wheat, use rice flour instead of plain flour.

Make sure you check the label of your chicken broth to be sure it is soya free!

1. Cut the chicken breasts into 2.5-centimetre (1-inch) cubes on the chopping board with the chef's knife.

2. Heat the oil in a frying pan on the hob on medium-high. Add the chicken and use the tongs to flip and stir. Cook about five minutes, or until no longer pink inside. Remove from heat and set aside.

3. Clean your knife and chopping board. Then chop the onion and celery into small pieces and set aside.

4. Add the butter to the large stockpot and melt over medium heat.

5. Put the onion and celery in the pot and stir gently. Allow to cook for about three to four minutes, or until the vegetables begin to soften.

6. Sprinkle the flour over the vegetables and stir until absorbed into the butter.

7. Pour in the chicken broth and milk, and stir quickly.

8. Increase the heat to medium-high until the stew begins to bubble softly. Reduce the heat to medium.

9. Add the frozen vegetables, salt, pepper and the cooked chicken to the pot.

10. Cook for 30 minutes before serving.

CHICKEN CRANBERRY SALAD
LETTUCE WRAPS

Crispy lettuce makes the perfect package for delicious ingredients in these tasty wraps! Mix in a tangy homemade sauce to go with your scrumptious meal.

Preparation time: 15 minutes

Cooking time: 5 minutes

Makes 4 wraps

Ingredients

1 head round lettuce

1 chicken breast

1 tablespoon olive oil

1 Granny Smith apple

1 celery stalk

175 grams olive oil mayonnaise

½ teaspoon honey

½ teaspoon Dijon mustard

60 grams dried cranberries

1 teaspoon salt

Tools

kitchen roll

chopping board

chef's knife

frying pan

measuring spoons/scales

tongs

mixing bowl

spoon

Allergen alert!

Read the label of your mayonnaise carefully to ensure it does not include any allergens you are avoiding.

Dried cranberries are commonly manufactured with nuts, so it's important to check with the manufacturer.

1. Carefully pull off about 8 leaves of lettuce. Rinse well and dry with kitchen roll. Set aside.

2. Cut the chicken breast into 2.5-centimetre (1-inch) cubes. Add the oil to the frying pan and heat on the hob on medium.

3. Add the chicken and turn the pieces with tongs. Cook until no longer pink inside. When the chicken is done, set aside in the frying pan to cool almost completely.

4. Clean your chopping board and knife. Then chop the apple into 1.3-centimetre (½-inch) cubes and discard the core.

5. Chop the celery into 1.3-centimetre (½-inch) pieces.

6. Add the apple, celery, mayonnaise, honey, mustard, cranberries and salt to a mixing bowl. Stir to combine.

7. When the chicken has cooled, add it to the mixing bowl and toss lightly until coated.

8. To assemble the wraps, stack two lettuce leaves on top of each other. Spoon about a quarter of the chicken salad in the centre. Fold the sides in and roll at the same time to envelop the filling.

9. Serve cold, and store leftovers in the refrigerator for up to three days.

CHEF'S TIP

Try using mango, pineapple or grapes instead of apple. Raisins, dates or dried apricots can be used instead of dried cranberries.

GREEK TURKEY BURGERS
WITH CUCUMBER TZATZIKI

Forget the traditional burger!
Go Greek by adding a cool and
refreshing cucumber tzatziki
sauce to a turkey burger.

Preparation time: 15 minutes

Cooking time: 15 minutes

Makes 4 burgers

Ingredients

Cucumber tzatziki

½ cucumber

1 clove garlic

60 millilitres coconut cream

1 teaspoon lemon juice

¼ teaspoon salt

⅛ teaspoon ground black pepper

Turkey burgers

2 cloves garlic

a handful of fresh oregano leaves

1 lemon

1 teaspoon salt

½ teaspoon ground black pepper

680 grams turkey mince

1 tablespoon olive oil

4 slices pitta bread

Tools

chopping board

chef's knife

grater

2 mixing bowls

measuring spoons/scales/jug

micro-grater

frying pan

spatula

Allergen alert!

Read the pitta bread label carefully
to make sure it is certified soya free.

If you are avoiding wheat, make sure you choose
a variety that uses an alternative type of flour too.

1. For the tzatziki, cut the cucumber in half lengthwise. Then scoop out the seeds with a spoon. Grate half of the cucumber and place in a mixing bowl. Set aside the other half.

2. Chop one clove of garlic finely and place in a mixing bowl. Add the coconut cream, lemon juice, salt and pepper to the mixing bowl. Stir to combine and store in refrigerator until ready to use.

3. For the burgers, chop two cloves of garlic finely and toss in a mixing bowl.

4. Pull the leaves off of the fresh oregano and chop lightly. Add to bowl.

5. Zest the yellow part of the lemon peel using the micro-grater over the mixing bowl.

6. Add the salt, ground pepper and turkey mince to the bowl. Mix gently with your hands until all ingredients are evenly mixed.

7. Divide the meat into 4 evenly-shaped balls. Flatten into round patties.

8. Heat the oil in the frying pan over medium heat. Carefully place the patties in the hot oil, avoiding splashes.

9. Cook about six minutes on each side, or until no longer pink inside. Use the spatula for flipping.

10. To assemble the burgers, open the pitta bread and slide a burger in. Then place 2 tablespoons of the tzatziki on top of each burger.

11. Serve immediately.

SESAME BEEF SKEWERS

Typical Asian cuisine uses soya as a key
ingredient. But you can still enjoy a
similar soya flavour with coconut aminos!
Give your beef skewers a zingy Asian
flare with this easy recipe.

Preparation time: 1 hour 15 minutes
 (1 hour inactive)

Cooking time: 4 minutes

Makes 12 skewers

Ingredients

450 grams flank steak

2 cloves garlic

2 spring onions

2.5-cm piece of fresh ginger

60 millilitres coconut aminos

2 tablespoons chilli-garlic sauce

2 tablespoons toasted sesame oil

1 tablespoon rice wine vinegar

cooking spray

Tools

chopping board

chef's knife

mixing bowl

micro-grater

measuring spoons/scales/jug

whisk

large resealable bag

12 wooden skewers

baking tray

foil

1. Using the chopping board and chef's knife, cut the flank steak into long, 1.3-centimetre (½-inch) thick strips. Set aside.

2. Clean your chopping board and knife. Then chop the garlic and spring onions into very small pieces and set aside.

3. Using the micro-grater, carefully grate the ginger over a chopping board. Add it to the mixing bowl, along with the garlic and onions.

4. Add the coconut aminos, chilli-garlic sauce, sesame oil and vinegar to the mixing bowl. Whisk until mixed.

5. Place the marinade and beef into a resealable bag. Using fingers, squish the beef until coated. Place the bag in the refrigerator for one hour.

6. Soak skewers in water while meat marinates.

7. Place the oven rack 10 to 15 cm (4 to 6 inches) below the grill. Set the grill on high. Line a baking tray with foil. Place a wire cooling rack on top of the foil and spray with cooking spray.

8. Thread the skewers through the slices of meat. Discard the leftover marinade.

9. Place the skewers on the wire cooling rack. Then set the baking tray in the oven.

10. Use tongs to turn over the skewers after two minutes. Cook an additional two minutes.

11. Remove from the oven and allow to cool for five minutes before serving hot.

Allergens eradicated!

No major food allergens found here!

19

ASIAN NOODLES

Looking for a quick and easy Eastern-inspired dish to complement your meal? Savoury noodles and crunchy vegetables provide flavour without soya!

Preparation time: 15 minutes

Cooking time: 10 minutes

Serves 4

Ingredients

225 grams rice noodles

2 cloves garlic

1 small onion

2 tablespoons oil, such as olive oil

255 grams fresh slaw

120 millilitres coconut aminos

1 teaspoon crushed ginger

1 teaspoon lime juice

2 teaspoons honey

Tools

saucepan

chopping board

chef's knife

frying pan

measuring spoons/scales/jug

spoon

1. Cook the rice noodles according to package directions and set aside.

2. Chop the garlic and onion into small pieces and set aside.

3. Heat oil in a frying pan over medium-high heat. Add the onion and garlic. Stir frequently to avoid burning. Cook for about two minutes, or until the onions start to soften.

4. Add the slaw, coconut aminos, ginger, lime juice and honey. Stir well. The sauce should begin to thicken.

5. Cook for about three minutes before adding the cooked rice noodles.

6. Stir frequently to avoid sticking.

7. Serve immediately.

CHEF'S TIP

This recipe is a wonderful side for the Sesame beef skewers.

Allergens eradicated!

No major food allergens found here!

CHEESY POPCORN

Ready to pop up a snack for film night? You can impress guests with this cheesy, soya-free popcorn!

Preparation time: 5 minutes

Cooking time: 30 minutes

Makes about 10 servings

Ingredients

60 grams popping corn

3 tablespoons olive oil

50 grams finely grated Parmesan cheese

Tools

large pan with lid

measuring spoons/scales

roasting tin

spoon

Allergen alert!

If you're avoiding dairy, leave the Parmesan and go for 2 tablespoons of nutritional yeast instead.

1. Preheat oven to 130°C.

2. In a large pan, place the popping corn and 1 tablespoon olive oil. Cover with a lid and set the hob to medium. Wait until the corn begins popping, and then remove from heat after a minute to avoid burning. Wait until you no longer hear popping, then remove the lid.

3. Pour the popcorn into the roasting tin. Drizzle with olive oil and Parmesan cheese. Stir with a spoon to make sure everything is coated.

4. Bake in the oven for 20 minutes, stirring after 10 minutes. The popcorn should be crispy and coated with cheese.

CHEF'S TIP

Store leftovers in small resealable bags for tasty snacks to grab on the go.

FRUIT LEATHERS

Reading the ingredients list of processed food can be overwhelming. There are dozens of ingredients, and most of them are too difficult to even pronounce! With only two ingredients, these fruit leathers are nutritious, delicious and soya free!

Preparation time: 5 minutes

Cooking time: 6 hours

Makes 24 servings

Ingredients

450 grams your favourite fruit

2 teaspoons honey

Tools

large baking tray

baking parchment

measuring spoons/scales

blender

spatula

pizza cutter

Allergens eradicated!

No major food allergens found here!

1. Preheat oven to 65°C. Line a baking tray with baking parchment and set aside.

2. If your fruit contains pits, stones or stems, remove them. Add fruit and honey to the blender. Blend on high until smooth.

3. Spread the blended mix evenly on the lined baking sheet and place in the oven.

4. Bake for six hours, or until the mixture no longer feels wet.

5. Remove from oven and let cool. Carefully peel the fruit leather away from the baking parchment. Use the pizza cutter to cut the fruit leather into strips. Place the strips on baking parchment or roll them up as they are.

6. Place in an airtight container for up to two weeks.

CHEF'S TIP

Need some fruit ideas? Strawberries, blueberries, peaches, pineapple, raspberries, grapes or bananas work well in this recipe!

CRISPY POTATO SLICES

AND DILL DIP

Skip the soya and make your own crispy, crunchy potato slices in the oven. Add a smooth and creamy dip with a dill-flavoured kick.

Preparation time: 10 minutes

Cooking time: 20 minutes

Serves 4

Ingredients

Crispy potato slices

1 large Russet potato

3 tablespoons olive oil

1 teaspoon salt

Dill dip

4 stems fresh dill

1 avocado

60 millilitres coconut cream

2 tablespoons lemon juice

1 teaspoon dehydrated onion

½ teaspoon salt

Tools

large baking tray

baking parchment

chopping board

chef's knife

pastry brush

spatula

kitchen roll

measuring spoons/jug

mixing bowl

fork

Allergen alert!

Coconut is classified as a fruit. But if you have a tree nut allergy, please talk to your doctor before eating it.

1. Preheat oven to 200°C. Line a baking tray with baking parchment and set aside.

2. Carefully slice the potatoes about 0.3-centimetre (⅛-inch) thick or as thinly as you can.

3. Space them evenly on the baking tray. Make sure the pieces do not touch each other.

4. Brush both sides of each slice with olive oil. Then sprinkle with salt.

5. Place in oven and bake for 20 minutes or until golden brown.

6. Transfer slices to kitchen roll to absorb extra oil. Allow to cool before serving.

7. For the dip, pull the leaves off of the dill and chop into small pieces. Add to a mixing bowl.

8. Remove the skin and pit of the avocado and scoop the pulp into the mixing bowl. Mash with a fork.

9. Add the coconut cream, lemon juice, dehydrated onion and salt to the bowl. Stir until smooth.

10. Serve immediately with the potato slices.

11. Store leftovers in an airtight container in the refrigerator for up to three days.

CHOCOLATE DRIZZLE
RICE TREATS

Ready for dessert? Crispy and sweet, these rice treats can be a delectable finish to a soya-free meal.

Preparation time: 10 minutes

Cooking time: 1 hour (1 hour inactive)

Makes 24 squares

Ingredients

175 grams honey

115 grams sunflower seed butter

15 grams butter

100 grams puffed rice cereal

Chocolate drizzle

115 grams semi-sweet chocolate chips

1 teaspoon coconut oil

Tools

2 small saucepans

measuring spoons/scales

large mixing bowl

spatula

23 x 33-cm (9 x 13-in) baking tray

fork

chef's knife

1. Combine honey, sunflower seed butter, and butter in a small saucepan over medium heat. Allow the butter to melt. Mix well until runny.

2. Add the rice cereal to the mixing bowl. Pour the honey mixture in, stirring with a spatula to coat the cereal well.

3. Using the spatula, press the mixture into a baking tray and allow to cool.

4. While the rice cereal treats cool, make the drizzle. In a saucepan, combine the chocolate chips with the coconut oil over low heat. Stir frequently to avoid burning.

5. When the chips are melted, drizzle the chocolate over the treats with a fork.

6. Allow to cool completely and cut into 24 squares with the chef's knife.

7. Keep leftovers covered at room temperature for up to a week.

Allergen alert!

Check the labels and contact the manufacturers of your rice cereal and chocolate chips to make sure they are free of any allergens you are avoiding.

If you're avoiding dairy, make sure you use a butter substitute instead of normal butter.

Coconut is classified as a fruit. But if you have a tree nut allergy, please talk to your doctor before eating it.

PEACH AND BLUEBERRY
CRUMBLE

Let's get ready to crumble! Dual fruity flavours will tantalize your taste buds with this soya-free dessert. The crumbly topping provides a crunch but also melts in your mouth.

Preparation time: 15 minutes

Cooking time: 45 minutes

Serves 8

Ingredients

4 ripe peaches, fresh or frozen

295 grams blueberries, fresh or frozen

2 tablespoons lemon juice

2 tablespoons arrowroot powder

½ teaspoon ground cinnamon

75 grams rice flour

100 grams dark brown sugar

45 grams oats

55 grams cold butter

Tools

chopping board

chef's knife

2 mixing bowls

measuring spoons/scales

spatula

20 x 20-cm (8 x 8-in) baking dish

1. Preheat oven to 190°C.

2. Remove the pits from the peaches and cut into 0.6-centimetre (¼-inch) slices. Place in mixing bowl.

3. Add blueberries, lemon juice, arrowroot powder and cinnamon to the bowl and stir.

4. Pour the fruit into the bottom of a baking dish. Set aside.

5. In a second mixing bowl, combine the rice flour, brown sugar and oats. Set aside.

6. Cut the butter into tiny pieces and add to the bowl, then stir.

7. Sprinkle the topping over the peaches and blueberries.

8. Bake for about 45 minutes, or until the top is golden brown.

9. Cut into 8 pieces and serve warm.

CHEF'S TIP

If it isn't peach season, don't be afraid of frozen peaches. Frozen fruits and vegetables are picked at the peak of their season and frozen immediately. This keeps the freshness and nutrition packed inside. Just let them thaw, and then drain the liquid before you add them to your dish.

GLOSSARY

assemble put all the parts of something together

consume eat or drink something

discard throw something away because it is not needed

drizzle let a substance fall in small drops

mash smash a soft food into a lumpy mixture

pit single central seed or stone of some fruits

pulp soft juicy or fleshy part of a fruit or vegetable

slice cut into thin pieces with a knife

thaw bring frozen food to room temperature

whisk stir a mixture rapidly until it's smooth

READ MORE

Allergy-free Cooking for Kids, Pamela Clark (Sterling Epicure, 2014)

The Allergy-Free Family Cookbook, Fiona Heggie and Ellie Lux (Orion, 2015)

The Kids Only Cookbook, Sue Quinn (Quadrille Publishing, 2013)

WEBSITE

www.allergyuk.org
If you have any allergies, this is the website to go to. It provides
lots of useful information and a helpline.